F

Free Radio & Podcast Marketing in 30 Minutes

"No matter what you sell, getting PR is critical for spreading the word. Today podcasts are as important as radio and this book is the best I've seen that handles both."

—Martin Yate, author, *New York Times* bestseller
Knock 'em Dead: The Ultimate Job Search Guide

"Jim has given you the keys to the kingdom with this book! He breaks down the branding and booking process into easily accomplishable steps that can help almost anyone get booked on radio and podcasts. I hope my clients never see this book!"

—Wendy Guarisco, founder, Guarisco Group PR Agency

"If anybody knows about how to turn a radio show into revenue for your business, it's Jim Beach. This book shares the secrets he's learned by doing this for his own business over a decade. Pure gold."

—Jamie Turner, author, speaker, and CEO, 60SecondMarketer.com

"Jim's book is packed with nuggets on how to secure radio or podcast interviews to market your business. I've used many of his strategies in the past and they have worked well for me. I highly recommend checking it out— you'll get a very good ROI on your investment."

—Jason Treu, executive coach and #1 best-selling author, *Social Wealth*

Free Radio & Podcast
Marketing

In **30** Minutes

Fire your publicist and leverage free radio and podcasting to market your business, brand, or idea

Jim Beach WITH Rachel Lewyn

IN 30 MINUTES® Guides

PUBLISHED BY i30 MEDIA CORPORATION
Newton, Massachusetts

Contents

Contents

PART 5: Pre-interview preparation

PART 6: How to give a great interview

PART 7: The aftermath

Foreword

Isn't it amazing, in an age of tweets and likes and "digital disruption" and other fancy buzzwords, that the spoken word still commands so much power?

Indeed, despite the popularity of smartphones and other screen-based entertainment, AM/FM radio still has the greatest reach of any medium. According to Nielsen, more than 90% of adults—including young adults aged 18–34—are reached by radio every week. Radio's younger sibling, podcasting, is also gaining in strength, with more than 60 million U.S. households being fans of at least one podcast.

Wouldn't it be great to leverage the power of radio and podcasting, to establish your brand, tell your story, spread your ideas, or promote a new product or business you're working on?

In the next half-hour, you're going to learn how to do just that. Your guides are Jim Beach and Rachel Lewyn, authors of *Free Radio & Podcast Marketing In 30 Minutes*. Jim is an experienced broadcaster and entrepreneur. At the age of 25, he started a computer education business that he grew to $12 million in annual revenue before it was acquired. His small business radio show, School for Startups Radio, airs on 16 AM/FM stations and online. Rachel has experience as a radio producer and digital content creator for entertainment website FanBolt.

Nearly anyone can use their ideas to get on the air. Consider the following examples:

➤ **Sandra and Jason are founders of a company** that makes backpacks, tents, and other camping equipment. In the past, the two founders hired a national marketing agency and used social media and blog posts to highlight new products, but were disappointed with the results. To get the word out about a new line of tents, they want to ditch the expensive marketing agency and try some of the specialist podcasts devoted to camping and the outdoors, as well as radio shows focusing on entrepreneurship.

➤ **Ray is running for state senator**, but doesn't have a budget for a television ad campaign. He wonders how to entice local radio talk shows to have him appear as a guest to talk about issues that are important to the electorate.

➤ **Fabiana has just completed work on her latest book**, a nonfiction title about adoption. She has a lot of information to share, not to mention stories about parents and children who have come together despite many obstacles. She thinks radio would be an ideal platform to share these stories and promote the book, but doesn't know where to start ... and can't afford a professional publicist.

➤ **Jessica recently retired from a Hollywood marketing firm**, and now wants to embark on a second career as a public speaker and consultant. She is a natural in front of audiences, and believes that her marketing framework and war stories from the entertainment world would go over well with radio and podcast audiences.

➤ **Benson is an activist** who is passionate about a local wilderness area under threat from commercial development. He has assembled a small group of supporters that includes birders, deer hunters, farmers, and hikers. Benson believes radio coverage of the group could help expand support and build awareness of this issue.

You may have a similar cause, product, campaign, or brand that you want to promote to radio and podcast audiences. In the past, it may have been necessary to hire a publicist to get in front of broadcast producers or programming staff, at a cost of thousands of dollars per month. Or, you would have to lean on media connections to get on the air.

Now it's possible for nearly anyone with a message or story to book guest appearances and interviews, whether it's a niche podcast with an audience of just a few hundred people or a national program that reaches millions. Jim and Rachel have put together a guide to doing it right, from conducting research to writing pitches to taking part in engaging discussions with hosts.

This book, like all IN 30 MINUTES guides, is designed to be read in a single sitting. After you are done reading, be sure to check out the companion website at schoolforstartupsradio.com where you can sign up for Jim's mailing list and access bonus chapters and other goodies.

We only have 30 minutes, so let's get started!

Ian Lamont

Founder, IN 30 MINUTES guides

Introduction

What is it about the radio medium that makes it uniquely qualified to sell your product and get you free publicity?

Before I get into that, it's important to note that while this book concentrates on radio, all of the strategies are equally applicable to podcasts. The methodology is exactly the same.

One of my favorite things about using radio as a marketing tool is its incredibly **broad, diverse applicability**. Chapter 1 will expand on that, but in the meantime, I want to emphasize that no matter your company's niche, no matter the nature of your product, the tactics in this book will substantially benefit you. Part of that applicability is the sheer breadth of radio's audience, and the variability inherent within that audience. Almost everyone listens to radio.

Don't believe me?

Radio has the broadest reach of any media platform. Terrestrial radio— that's your traditional AM/FM broadcast, the kind of stuff you listen to during your car ride to work—reaches nearly the entire U.S. population. According to data compiled by Nielsen and Pew, 93% of Americans listen to terrestrial radio. That's higher than TV viewership (89%), smartphone use (83%), and use of other media devices.

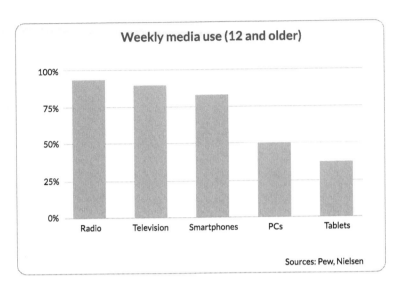

Weekly media use (12 and older)

Sources: Pew, Nielsen

Of the 271 million Americans over the age of 12 listening to radio every week, some 67 million are millennials—the highly valued young adult demographic that drives trends and buying patterns. When it comes to radio formats, talk/information-based radio is one of the most popular genres, second only to top 40 contemporary pop radio.

Digital radio/online streaming is also among the most listened-to formats for broadcasting, and listenership has exploded in the past few years. Recent data by Edison Research and Triton Digital found that 57% of Americans aged 12+ had listened to online radio in the past month, while 50% had listened in the past week. In 2017, those numbers grew to 61% and 53%, respectively—a pretty hefty jump for just one year.

If you approach radio and podcasting the right way (by following the system outlined in this book), it's inherently self-sustainable and will serve you well for years into the future. Every appearance lays the groundwork for the next, and every interview expands the scope of your audience and thus your potential to get real results, whether it's sales, awareness of an issue, or some other benefit.

Protip: Radio has immense potential to reach listeners of every sensibility, and new ways to tune in are constantly emerging. It's an incredibly exciting time for the medium—the possibilities are boundless.

Part 1

Why radio?

CHAPTER 1

Marketing you can afford

One of the greatest things about the radio business is its astounding topical diversity.

If you're skeptical, I'm not surprised. I hear it all the time. "There just aren't any shows in my particular niche," the skeptics say. "Nobody's going to want to listen to me talk about antique lamps!"

The skeptics are wrong. Those wildly niche audiences are out there in droves. I don't care what you're selling, or which crowd you're trying to reach. Whether it's gardening, parenting, sailboats, paranormal activity, or whatever, I promise there are innumerable shows out there just waiting to help boost you, your product, and your brand to the next level.

Take a quick look at the list below. It represents a small selection of radio categories in which 100 shows or more exist. 100 shows or *more*! Addiction, animals, science fiction, sex, art and design, beauty and fashion, business and finance, cars, crime, disability, entertainment, environment, food and wine, gardening, LGBTQ, health and fitness, history, labor, law, military, nautical ...

The list, obviously, goes on. That's over 100 shows about *sailing*, people! I live in Atlanta—10 different radio shows exist about Atlanta alone. How many are there about your city?

Addiction	Disabilities	Men	Relationships
African American	Food/Wine	Outdoors	Science
Animals	Gardening	Paranormal	Science Fiction
Art/Design	LGBTQ	Parenting	Self Help
Beauty/Fashion	Health/Fitness	Politics	Seniors
Business/Finance	History	Pregnancy	Sex
Cars	Law	Publishing	Sports
Entertainment	Military	Real Estate	Technology
Environment	New Age	Regional	Travel
Crime	Nautical	Religion	Women

Do any of these categories appeal to your business? Would one of these shows help sell your product, or boost your brand? My guess is yes. *That's the power of radio.* There are loads of shows on which you and the thing you want to promote would make perfect guests. That is, loads of individual platforms to accelerate your sales and maximize exposure for your brand.

Podcasting takes niche programming to the next level. As of this writing, the top 50 podcasts according to Stitcher (a popular app for listening to podcasts) include shows about the following topics:

History	Religion	Sports
Politics	Medicine	Pop culture
Law	True crime	Personal finance

So when it comes to free radio and podcast PR, don't cop out with the old "no shows in my category" excuse. The shows are most definitely there.

Airtime is expensive

Let's compare the bare numbers and costs of free PR versus conventional advertising methods. How much money can you actually save by ditching expensive ad budgets and taking the marketing road less traveled?

Here are the facts: As of this writing, 30 seconds of airtime on Atlanta's 8th most popular radio station costs $380. The #1 radio station in Los Angeles, KFI, charges $12,000 for 60 seconds during peak drive time. Rates for the king of radio, Howard Stern, run into the tens of thousands of dollars for 60 seconds of commercial time.

Now, let's say you were able to get on that same station, KFI in Los Angeles, for a five-minute interview. That's equivalent to $60,000 in free advertising. Even better, listeners will be far more inclined to listen to an interview as opposed to an ad. On top of that, your relevance and credibility as a source is increased simply by virtue of being on the show. It's a transfer of trust scenario. People won't just listen to you—they might even believe you! It's an infinitely better deal all the way around.

SEO your way to the top

Do you know what they call someone whose name pops up as the #1 search result on Google?

A millionaire.

And why do those names show up at the top of Google? Three letters: SEO.

SEO stands for *search engine optimization*—fancy terminology for how high your name, website, or business appears on search engines like Google or Bing. The higher your web page's ranking, the easier it is for folks to find your company. Needless to say, SEO carries a lot of weight in terms of exposure and credibility, and the goal is always to hit number one.

In the past, some slick online brands have paid big money for thousands of phony links leading back to their own web pages, fooling search engines and creating false buzz around the content. But Google has smartened up in the past few years and has taken steps toward preventing this kind of trickery.

Radio and podcasts, on the other hand, are extremely effective unsung heroes when it comes to boosting search engine results. Let's say I get on a radio show for free. What are the producers going to do? They're going to post a little page about me, likely with a short bio, a picture, and a link to my website (see sample, below). This is just standard procedure at many radio and podcast programs.

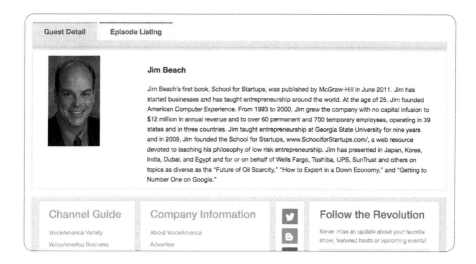

That little link is your ticket. Getting inbound links from such programs will dramatically increase your search engine score—one of the main reasons why radio and podcast appearances are so advantageous to you, your company, or your brand.

On a basic level, two things affect your search engine scores: the number of links bouncing around the Internet that lead to your site, and the quality of those links. Reputation is obviously a major pillar of SEO—lots of sound links leading to your page convince Google that your business produces fresh, popular content, and your scores will grow accordingly.

Other factors that may boost website ranking

- Regularly updated content
- Content that loads quickly
- SSL-enabled hosting (https://)
- Content that looks good and renders quickly on mobile devices
- Properly configured sitemaps
- No broken links or website errors
- No links to suspicious domains or malware

Land 200 free interviews and you could also land up to 200 free links, all associated with high-quality sources. Popular shows enjoy formidable search engine rankings themselves—and by appearing as a guest, you can piggyback off of those numbers and maximize your own! When a show creates links to your content, you gain terrific face time not only with the show's existing listeners, but also with Google's SEO algorithms.

Amassing search engine links from strong, reputable websites is essential, and there's no better way to do it than leveraging radio and podcast appearances. This is an extremely effective and inexpensive strategy to push your site to the top of Google. Lots of interviews means lots of links. Lots of links leads to lots of sales!

CHAPTER 2

Building credibility

No matter what product you're selling, no matter what idea you're promoting, credibility is the foundation upon which all other aspects of your pitch will rest. On a daily basis, the average American is inundated with a never-ending stream of superfluous and/or questionable information in the form of Internet ads, telemarketing calls, fast-food commercials, and other marketing dreck. Savvy consumers have grown increasingly intolerant of the B.S.

What this means for you is that, as a person with something to sell, credibility is king. Radio and podcasting present an extremely effective way to build this credibility with little or no spending on your part.

Every time you appear as a radio or podcast guest, your credibility builds. Every time you are interviewed, you become a greater expert. I may not be able to claim expertise on any one topic—but do you know what I *can* say? "Well, I appeared on CNN, and they called me 'the Simon Cowell of small business.'" Those six words in themselves made me a bigger expert, and they have served me well ever since.

Showcasing your expertise

Let's talk about expertise.

Representing yourself as a guru in your field will be instrumental in enhancing your value to producers as a promising guest, as well as your ability to gain respect and attention from listeners off the bat. Remember, this whole "getting on the air" thing is designed to solidify your status as an expert so that people will buy your products, connect with your brand, or recognize your ideas.

Great news—radio shows and podcasts *love* expert guests. Hosting expert guests is what lends shows *their* credibility.

Think about it. If the show has horrible guests, the show looks bad. If the show has great guests—qualified individuals with clout in their industry—the show looks great. The host looks great. The producer looks great. So these programs spend a lot of time searching for experts.

I want you to position yourself as a leading expert in whatever field you choose. For instance:

➤ If you're a gold sales expert, that's your angle.

➤ If you know all there is to know about clowning and its incredible psychological benefits for children, then you're an expert on that.

➤ If you know how to make the best cider with locally grown apples, then that's the expertise you want to bring to the show.

➤ If you're a politician with the best understanding of local tax policies, lead with that.

The important thing is to represent yourself and your personal brand in a way that makes the audience and the host and the producer think, "Wow! This person really knows what he/she is talking about!"

So, when you're trying to land a spot on a show, there are a few different ways you can establish yourself as a pro. You could say:

> *"I'm a great parent and educator, and 3,000 people have completed my parenting class. More than 95% reported that their infants were able to sleep through the night by the time they were two months old. I want to be on your show—my expert advice can really help new parents in your audience."*

There you go—you specialize in getting babies to sleep, and you establish that with an impressive statistic reinforcing your pitch.

Or maybe you could say:

> *"I went to Harvard, and I have my Ph.D., from the University of Michigan. I have published more than 25 scholarly papers and three books on invasive plant species. I am truly an expert in my field, and I want to be on your show."*

Any information that substantiates your credentials is information you need to share. Whether it's your education, past sales, past successes, or other shows that you've appeared on, demonstrating your value as an informed and competent professional is the name of the game.

When I appear on a local radio show, I like to email all of the other hosts in the area with a link to my segment. It's my way of giving them a little nudge. "Look—this guy thought I was an expert! See how well I did on his show? I'll do just as well on yours."

Protip: Whether it's through your credentials, your words, or your actions, expertise should be coming out of your ears. Asserting your credibility in this way is a hugely advantageous prerequisite to securing interviews and wowing the audience.

CHAPTER 3

Why hosts have guests

Ever wonder exactly why radio and podcast hosts have guests in the first place?

There are some radio hosts—Rush Limbaugh, for example—who almost never have guests. That's really hard to do, people! Think about it—can you talk *and* be entertaining for *three hours*, nonstop? It's an extraordinarily difficult feat.

I have my own radio show. I am on-air six days per week for one hour each day. I'll let you in on a trade secret: Scraping together enough material to talk about for that long is actually really tough. You might think that folks in this line of work can talk to anyone, about anything, for any length of time, but it's not as easy as it sounds.

It stands to reason that most hosts rely on guests to make the show better. A two-way conversation is almost always more engaging than a monologue, and guests create an ideal opportunity for such conversations.

News cycles and current events also generate an extremely convenient opening for experts in a given industry. If there's something interesting happening in the news, the host's natural inclination is to have an expert appear on the show and offer knowledgeable commentary. Beyond this, hosts also rely on guests for education, entertainment, and all things that make radio and podcasts worth listening to.

The most important takeaway from this chapter is that hosts have wide expanses of time to fill up. I'll let you in on another secret: Hosts are absolutely *desperate* for guests. Desperate! I have to interview 14 different people every single week. I spend more time finding guests than I do editing and preparing the show. Finding guests is the hardest part of radio and podcast programming, bar none.

And that's where you come in. Out of the blue, you are going to burst into this host's life and dazzle him/her with your valuable know-how and charming anecdotes. That's exactly why they're going to want you on the show.

I emphasize the desperation of hosts not to insinuate that they will take anyone they can get (they certainly will not). Rather, I want to illustrate the enormous opportunity here for informative, captivating experts like YOU! I want to emphasize yet again that there are countless quality radio shows and podcasts out there just dying to benefit from your content.

Information and entertainment

Every time you appear on a radio show or podcast, you strike an implicit deal with the host. The host wants you on air for two reasons:

1. **You are informational.** You were invited on the show as an expert, and your interview will be packed with useful content, tips, tricks, and knowledge to be shared. "Do you want to know how to keep your kid sleeping soundly through the night? Come and listen to this interview—we'll tell you all about it!"

2. **You provide entertainment value.** The second reason hosts want you on their shows is for entertainment. Lots of segments are designed to be purely entertaining, and everyone knows that makes for some great radio.

But let's face it—it can be difficult to enthrall audiences while presenting as an expert on a given subject. If I'm an expert on property law, it is unlikely that I will enchant the hearts and minds of listeners based on the strength of my content. Property law is not, generally speaking, a subject ripe with potential for comic relief.

So, unless you are the Chris Rock of property law, I don't want you to rely too heavily on providing entertainment. However, if you're quick on your feet and great with cracking jokes, that's terrific! Crack away.

Even if you're not a natural comedian, it's possible to use pre-planned, humorous anecdotes to connect with the host and audience. Your listeners don't necessarily need to drop to the floor laughing, but some funny stories sprinkled throughout the segment will go a long way. I'll talk more about storytelling in Chapter 18.

Protip: It's important to remember that your principal draw as a guest is the valuable knowledge and expertise you share with the audience. Focus on the information first.

Part 2

Finding interview opportunities

CHAPTER 4

PR firms and publicists

The traditional way to get on the radio is by hiring a publicist. I've done this many times myself.

Back in 1999, I wanted to impress my mother. I was working with a high-quality publicist at the time. Her name was Jessica. With relatively low expectations, I called up my publicist and told her, "I want a fancy award in one of these business magazines. Is there any way you can get me in one of those '40 Under 40'-type things?"

Would you believe it—Jessica got back to me within 10 minutes: "Sure thing, Jim. That'll be $5,000."

That's right. Many personalities you see featured in those glossy articles—the top 100 entrepreneurs of the year, 50 up-and-coming CEOs you need to know—paid to get placed on the list!

Prior to this transaction, I was content in the romantic illusion that reporters go into the field each year, clipboard in hand, scouring the nation's entrepreneurs and ranking top contenders. But that's just not how these things work. There is no clipboard, no scouring, no meticulous investigation of our country's entrepreneurial rising stars. Publicists pay big bucks to get you on those lists, and you pay them big bucks to make it happen.

There is an important lesson to be learned here about the publicity industry, and where your business strategy fits into it. Publicists are tasked with getting you publicity, whether it's appearing on an important-sounding list, getting profiled in a glossy magazine, or being interviewed on the radio.

There is not a publicist in America (of any quality) who is cheaper than $2,500 per month. Can you afford that? Way back in the '90s, my company could afford that. But my current business will not support such a hefty monthly expenditure, and I'm willing to guess that yours won't either. It just doesn't make any financial sense.

Some publicists will charge on a per-placement basis. They'll say, "I'm going to try to get you a slot on CNN or MSNBC, and if I'm successful, I'll charge you $500." So you only pay for success.

It sounds like a pretty great deal, right? It sounds like a deal I would make all day long—as a matter of fact, I *have* made that deal all day long. Over the last decade, I've worked with 7 or 8 different publicists on a per-placement basis.

Do you want to know how many of those deals came through? Zero. Not a single one of my myriad per-placement publicity offers has ever materialized into an appearance on CNN, a magazine feature, or a *New York Times* interview. If the whole "paying for success" bargain seems too good to be true, that's because it usually is.

In other words, this arrangement offers false hope. That leaves traditional publicity methods involving an expensive monthly retainer—and that *still* doesn't guarantee anything! Your Jessica could work all month long, get you no placements whatsoever, and you will still owe her thousands of dollars for absolutely nothing.

How are you going to feel when you write her that check? That heart-sinking, baffled feeling is the reason why I do not hire publicists anymore.

Of course, there are a handful of publicists who can score a national TV appearance or placement in the *New York Times* for their clients. Perhaps one in 50 professional publicists have the necessary media connections and solid history that enable their clients to make these top-tier media appearances. You can bet that they are extremely selective about the clients they take on—and they will charge a lot for the privilege.

From this point forward, everything that I'm going to talk about assumes that you are not going down the traditional PR rabbit hole. It's too expensive, and the results are too uncertain.

And guess what—you don't need traditional PR! You can accomplish all of your publicity goals without ever giving Jessica a call, without ever blindly shelling out $2,500 on a leap of faith.

CHAPTER 5

Contacting producers vs. contacting hosts

In the chapters that follow, I sometimes talk about producers and hosts interchangeably. But there is an important distinction to be made between the two:

➤ The host's job is to be the face and voice of the program.

➤ The producer's job is to work behind the scenes and make the show happen.

Don't be fooled—oftentimes, the producer is far more important than the host. The producer is frequently the one who actually owns the show, and the host is merely a paid employee.

This has implications for your outreach efforts. Sometimes, seeking an invitation onto a show exclusively through the host can backfire. The host might say, "Yeah, I'd love to have you on the show." Then, he/she will email the producer, the producer will say no, and your chances are shot. You've simply gone about it the wrong way.

In many cases, producers like to have the final say on guests—it's their decision, and they can override hosts. This is especially true on larger programs. As audience size increases, the importance of the producer climbs accordingly.

So when you're building your list of potential targets, conduct two separate searches. Let's say you're a cooking expert—search "Cooking Radio Show Host" in one window and "Cooking Radio Show Producers" in another. You're going to get two different lists. I urge you to go through the producer whenever possible, because that's really how they want you to do it. You're less likely to step on any toes or hurt any feelings, and you're more likely to actually get on the show.

CHAPTER 6

Finding the right shows through marketplaces and lists

There are a number of ways to connect with the people who operate radio shows and podcasts. The resources described in this chapter allow program staff to connect with experts like you using special online marketplaces or published lists.

Online marketplaces provide worthwhile opportunities to connect with hosts, executive producers, and other folks who are—remember—desperate for quality guests. Let me tell you firsthand: Hosts and producers really do comb through these sources to find interesting guests, and they really will call or email you to put you on the show.

Some of the resources listed below are fantastic. I often turn to them to find guests for my own show.

RadioGuestList.com

One of my favorite ways to find new guests for my show is a nifty little site called **RadioGuestList.com**.

As you've probably gathered at this point in the book, the radio business yields publicity opportunities that are mutually beneficial to hosts and guests alike. Resources such as RadioGuestList.com and others like it are great demonstrations of this conveniently two-way street. As a reservoir of fresh interviewees, these sites serve me very well. As a potential guest looking for PR coverage, they will serve you just as well.

If you explore RadioGuestList.com, you will see thousands of radio and podcast hosts advertising for guests. Sometimes they'll even tell you what type of guest they're looking for—a paranormal expert who has actually seen a ghost firsthand, or an education guru with teaching experience in the American university system. But on the flip side, *you* can post too, advertising yourself as a potential guest.

Radio Interview Guest Request Alerts Premium Email Services

How to get on radio shows? Join our Premium email service to get more and better radio and podcast interview opportunities!

You can get 50% - 100% MORE Guest Requests delivered right to your inbox!

All THREE of our Premium email services can help you get MORE radio and podcast publicity because they include many Guest Request Alerts that our *free subscribers never receive.*

Getting ALL our interview opportunities delivered makes it **easier and quicker for you to get more free radio interviews** in your field of expertise, plus they support our service so we can keep delivering more of the publicity leads that your business needs.

All newsletters include a 10 Day FREE TRIAL! - Cancel Anytime.

3 Premium Options for You Below:

Please support our service by *upgrading* from our free email service to choose:

This site has a few packages. I pay about $30 per month to get listed on this service, and I have gotten placements and good interviews because of it. I probably get about two interviews per month from RadioGuestList.com, and consider the monthly subscription to be well worth the price.

RTIR and RadioSpace.com

There are other resources that take a similar approach. Another one I like is called **Radio Television Interview Report (RTIR)**.

RTIR is an electronic publication released twice per week on www.RTIR. com. It's basically the same concept as RadioGuestList.com—hosts can post ads for guests, and guests can post ads for hosts. Again, it is a convenient and productive resource for everybody involved.

A fantastic site in the same vein is **RadioSpace.com**, which conveniently separates radio shows and additional databases by genre.

Going for the big guns with Talkers.com

If your heart is set on landing a spot on huge national radio shows, check out **Talkers.com**.

This site is a good resource for the big players—the national shows and celebrity hosts that everyone has heard of. Talkers.com allows experts to advertise their services just like the sites mentioned above, but it's also where you'll go to find telephone numbers and emails of producers that work on A-level programs. Make no mistake—these shows are very difficult to get onto, but if you're going to try for the big leagues, this is the place to start.

HARO

The final site I want to recommend is a little bit different from the rest. It's called **HARO**, which stands for "Help A Reporter Out."

According to its website, HARO is "the most popular sourcing service in the English-speaking world, connecting journalists and bloggers with relevant expert sources." In other words, reporters writing articles post on this website requesting professional commentary on particular topics.

Let's say I'm a cryptocurrency expert—I log on to HARO, and I see that a reporter from the *New York Times* is writing an article about Bitcoin. They need an expert who can comment on the relationship between the depreciation of gold versus the appreciation of Bitcoin. All I have to do is email the reporter saying, "Hey, I'm available. I'd love to be part of your article. How can I help?"

More than 50,000 journalists and bloggers use HARO to find sources for their content. There is no shortage of articles that need input from specialists in a diverse range of subjects.

Go on HARO every day and look for posts relevant to your field of expertise. You can also join the HARO mailing list, which sends updates on potential openings up to 4 times per day.

The magical ingredient that makes HARO so effective (and thus a precious opportunity for you) is the transient nature of our daily news cycle. Think about it—these reporters are almost always on a deadline. They only have a certain amount of time (often just a couple of hours) before their stories are due to be published. This means that the site is perpetually in refresh mode, and new opportunities for sources are constantly pouring in. Every time you log in, there is potential for your name to appear in a major publication.

Transience is a bit of a double-edged sword, of course. If you see a request posted at 8 a.m., by the evening it's probably not worth responding to. But it's all about timing—if you can be one of the first two or three people to respond, and the people at the other end like what they see, your name is getting in that piece. You're going to get free publicity for it, and your credibility will develop with every article.

All of these sites are great ways to get your name on the radar of hosts, reporters, and others that can help you get free PR coverage and reinforce your position as the expert you want to be.

Published lists

My least favorite way to build a list of potential show targets is by simply buying a reference book or software program that does the work for you.

At first glance, these compilations may seem like the easiest and most convenient option. The authors have done all the work for you, right? All you have to do is make your way down the columns and pitch to each show one by one.

Not so fast! Considering the book publishing process typically takes about a year, these lists are composed at least 365 days before the books even hit the shelves, much less make it to your desk.

As noted earlier, the news industry is incredibly transient by nature. Parts are constantly in motion. Shows go defunct. New shows crop up. Producers and hosts are replaced. You might find producer Bob's phone number and email address in the reference book for this year, but by the following year, Andrea might be the producer of the program, with a completely different number and email address.

I have hosted my radio show for over two years now, and I am already on my fifth producer. I've burned through five producers in just *two* years! The turnover in this business is astounding. So keeping your target lists up-to-date is essential for accumulating contacts. An old list is just no good.

There are two exceptions to my no-compilations-allowed rule. The first is an author named Francine Silverman. She has published two high-quality books full of these lists—***Talk Radio Wants You,*** and ***Directory of Business Talk Radio Shows.***

Francine does a great job of grouping shows by category. There are pages and pages of entries for radio shows about parenting, military life, boating, pets, and so on. These books are great resources for finding top-notch shows to target, and I have used them myself with good results. She also runs a more regularly updated website, **TalkRadioAdvocate.com**. You'll find my show listed there.

My second exception is a man named Alex Carroll. You'll find Alex at **RadioPublicity.com**, where he runs a radio publicity program (surprise!) and maintains a database full of potential show targets.

The important distinction between Alex and Francine is that Alex's list is all about the big guys—the large-scale programs where you will inevitably be a small fish. The price of his program also runs fairly steep at a couple hundred dollars a pop—but if your priority is a quick and easy solution to the hunt for radio shows and podcasts, his site is one of the best.

These are both great resources that I used myself at the very beginning of my research, but I will say this: The strategies I've shared in this book will serve you far better. They're cheaper, they're current, and they're designed to serve the needs of guests and the needs of program staff.

CHAPTER 7

Finding programs using social media and search

I have built a target list of more than 2,000 radio show contacts, almost all of which pertain to business and entrepreneurship. The list includes contact information for the producers, hosts, and programs I want to pitch.

Sometimes, it's just a name and a telephone number. For many targets, I also include a website and an email address. In this chapter, I will discuss how I compiled this list using social media and search.

The three best social media platforms for building lists are LinkedIn, Twitter, and Facebook. Let's explore their strengths, their weaknesses, and the best ways to utilize them as resources for radio and podcast contacts. There will also be a discussion about augmenting your list with Google queries.

LinkedIn

LinkedIn has a great little search feature, but this site's largest drawback is its lack of specificity. If you open LinkedIn and type "Radio Host" into the search bar, you will be blasted with tens of thousands of results. Nobody has time to wade through that mess. You need to narrow things down.

So I like to cheat a little by using Google as a middleman. When I type "Entrepreneurship Radio Show" into a Google's advanced search feature, the query yields over 2,780 results—1,800 of which include LinkedIn posts or profiles. That's 1,800 potential targets for my list.

Are *all* of these results actually useable? Probably not. Some of them—perhaps about a third—mention entrepreneurship or radio shows in an unrelated or superfluous context. Google retrieves them largely by accident. But the other two-thirds should be good to go.

What do you do next? You visit each and every one of these links. You click on *every single one of them*. It may take hours. I try to knock out 100 per weekend.

Sometimes, you have to establish a network connection on LinkedIn before you can access an email address (select *Contact and Personal Info* on the target profile). Be sure to customize the invitation to increase your chances of being connected:

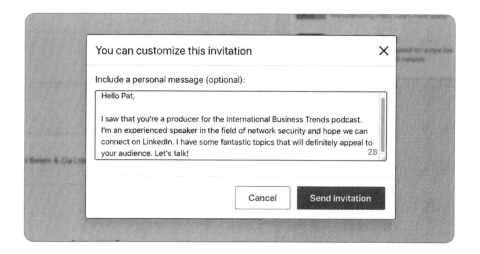

This is a touchy subject for LinkedIn—the site's policy warns against contacting people you do not already know.

But I do it anyway. I have reached out to thousands of strangers. It's gotten me kicked off of LinkedIn twice. I even had to go to LinkedIn school to be reinstated. Seriously, I'm not making this up! But you know what? It was worth it. I still connect with strangers in radio and podcasting all the time.

When you are reaching out to people you don't know, you can use a simple script that looks something like this:

"We've never met before, but I found you on LinkedIn. I think you're an interesting radio/podcast host. I think I'd be a great guest. Will you connect with me?"

Leave the message right there in the LinkedIn request form. Be sure to explain *why* you are reaching out to them. You may get kicked off of LinkedIn, but it is really not the end of the world. You can get reinstated, just like I was.

> **Protip:** LinkedIn also has a paid feature called InMail that lets you send messages to people who are not in your network. You may be able to access a free trial for LinkedIn's premium service, but otherwise expect to pay about $50 per month, billed annually.

Twitter

In my experience, Twitter yields an especially high rate of reply. I have about an 80% response rate from Twitter outreach efforts. It's a great resource when it comes to building lists.

The drawback: Twitter's search feature leaves a lot to be desired. It's shallow, lacks detail, and requires more time to wade through the results.

How do I go about connecting with hosts and producers through Twitter? I use a simple method:

1. Identify promising targets (this may take some time, owing to the search problem noted above).
2. Follow the accounts.
3. Scroll through their timelines and re-tweet interesting posts from the last week or so.
4. If a target tweets something the following day, I retweet that, too, or give it a "like."

People notice these things! They think, "Wow, I have a new person retweeting my tweets!" They might even feel warm and fuzzy inside. I believe Twitter is an inherently narcissistic platform, and this approach exploits that narcissism in a productive way.

A couple days later, I reach out to this person directly. I message him or her saying, "Hey—I really enjoy your tweets. I just learned about your radio/podcast show, and I think I'd make a great guest. I'd love to discuss this further with you." Boom! Another connection.

Facebook

Facebook search is quite useful for identifying targets. Pick a show/host/producer, follow his or her page or make a friend request, and then start sharing his or her material, setting yourself up to ask for a slot on the program.

This is a fantastic way to grow your list of targeted shows. Find your contacts, let them know you're paying attention, connect with them directly, and you're well on your way to building a robust list.

> **Protip:** If you are not familiar with how to use some of the social networks described above, check out *LinkedIn In 30 Minutes* and *Twitter In 30 Minutes*, which can help you get up to speed in no time.

Using Google to identify opportunities

At the risk of sounding obvious, Google is a great way to find radio shows, podcasts, hosts, and producers for your target list. It's almost too simple. If your expertise relates to boats or the ocean, just type "Nautical Radio Show" into the search bar, and thousands of links will flood your screen.

But here's something about Google you probably don't want to hear. You are not going to sift through the first 10 results and call it a day. You're not going to stop at the first 20, either. Ready? You're going to comb through the first *300* results or so. That's about 30 pages of results. After that 30-page mark, the data starts to wilt a little, and the good hits become sparse. But result number 297 might very well be a phenomenal radio show waiting to have you on as a guest.

You're not done yet. Phase two of the Google process will shake the tree further. Many shows have buttons or links that say, "Click here to become a guest!" After all, producers aren't hiding—they *want* you to find them, they *want* more and more guests to appear on the show.

Ever wonder what would happen if you were to type, "Become a guest" into the Google search bar? You will find hundreds of shows waiting for you to press that little "Click here" button. It's your invitation to connect with the producer directly—it's how you contact the show the way they *want* to be contacted.

Part 3

Getting the interview

CHAPTER 8

When to use email

Email can be a fantastic way to get on *some* radio shows and podcasts.

I once knew a guy named Jason—a distant acquaintance who happened to produce a fairly large radio show here in the Atlanta area. I recognized a great opportunity, and I decided to seize it by shooting him an email requesting a slot on the show.

It worked. I got on the show and had a great time on the program. After my segment, Jason thanked me for my time and told me, "I'm really glad I saw your email, Jim—that was a long shot!" Perplexed, I paused and asked him what he meant. How *should* I have approached him? "Well," he laughed, "the worst possible way is email, I can tell you that."

Here's the thing, folks. For a long, long time, emailing producers and hosts was the only method I used to get on radio or podcast programs. It's still my go-to way to pitch producers. Clearly, it has served me pretty well. And although Jason insisted that email is the worst strategy possible, it *did* get me on his show in the end, didn't it?

So, I want to take Jason's advice and add an important asterisk. I have found that his words of caution typically hold true for large-scale programs like his—shows with over 100,000 listeners. The bigger the show, the more cluttered the inbox, and the less likely it is that your email will be picked up amid the hundreds pouring in daily.

Email facts

- With the number of messages growing 4.4% per year, email inboxes are getting more and more crowded.
- Nearly half of recipients open email based on the subject line.
- Emails with 6-10 words in the subject line have the highest open rates.
- Emails with fancy fonts, images, or complex formatting are less likely to be read.
- Gmail has more than 1 billion active email users, compared to 400 million Outlook users.

Sources: Radicati, Invesp, Hubspot, Google, Microsoft

For shows with fewer than 100,000 listeners, however, email can absolutely be a viable approach to landing radio gigs. Keep this rule in mind as we further discuss using email to your advantage—pay attention to the scale of your targeted programs, and tailor your game plan accordingly.

I regularly use email to connect with producers and get on radio shows and podcasts. My close rate using this system averages about 15 to 20%. The best part? You can do this sitting on your sofa.

First, I sit at my computer and comb through LinkedIn, Twitter, Google, the works—compiling as many email addresses of hosts and producers that I can find. Once I am satisfied with the size of my pool, I start making the rounds, sending every email on the list a request to appear on their show. I try to send about 100 unsolicited requests per weekend—the whole process takes 7 or 8 hours.

After years of using this email system to make connections and appear on programs, I have amassed 2,000+ names of executive producers and hosts in the radio industry—particularly within the business radio niche.

What's in an email?

The attachments you include when emailing a show are an important aspect of landing an interview. Attachments typically include your bio, your headshot, your list of sample questions, and occasionally a press release to illustrate the subject you're talking about.

Generally, the larger the show, the lower the likelihood that staff will accept attachments. Pay attention! If you get no response from a program, that innocuous little paperclip icon might be the culprit (many companies' email systems automatically strip out attachments in order to reduce the risk of computer viruses).

Try sending another email without the attachment. If you did *not* send an attachment in the first place and received no response, try adding an attachment to your follow up email. Play around with both methods to see which works best with a given target.

Here is the good news: many programs love attachments from potential guests! Detailed bios, publicity photos, and other materials are a great way to illustrate who you are and what you do, all wrapped up in a neat little package. So let's deconstruct them.

I have two bios, which have the following structures:

1. The first bio is specifically designed as a mini-script from which the host reads as he or she introduces you on air. This little intro should be no longer than three lines of typed print—any longer than that is excessive and unnecessary.

2. The second bio should cover practically everything you've ever done. My second bio spans about two and a half pages. It even includes photos of things I have done, feats I have accomplished, important places my job has taken me. These longer bios should give the host/producer every detail they could possibly want about your life and expertise. Such details make the host more likely to connect with you and may also form the basis of questions during the interview.

Your bios will be significantly enhanced by the inclusion of hyperlinks to relevant online resources such as videos, product pages, or media mentions. Hyperlinks are a great way to reinforce noteworthy parts of your bio and provide producers with extra information about you.

For example, my bio says I have 275 interviews under my belt. In the actual email, "275 interviews" will be underlined and hyperlinked to the media section of my website, where there is a comprehensive list of every interview I've ever done. My bio also mentions that CNN once called me "the Simon Cowell of small business," so I like to insert a hyperlink leading to that CNN interview as well. Bio hyperlinks emphasize your credibility and serve as important resources for producers—use them!

It is also important to send a headshot. Radio shows and podcasts almost always post photos of their guests—wouldn't you rather feed producers a flattering picture of yourself than risk the dicey results of their dives through Google images?

Sample questions

Now, let's talk about sample questions. This list of questions serves as an outline for the interview, and it really does make things easier on everybody involved. Hosts do not want to spend unnecessary hours researching interviewees and pre-writing personalized questions. Throw them a bone.

Plus, sample questions reflect well on you as a guest! I always make sure to send my list to producers because it indicates that one, I am a professional, and two, this whole thing will be super easy for them.

For instance, if you were about to launch a new millennial-focused pizzeria chain, your list of sample questions might look something like this:

➤ What's the size of this market, and how much pizza does the average millennial eat in a year?

➤ How many millennials are there in your target markets?

➤ Where will your first 10 shops be located, and when will they open?

➤ What makes millennials different when it comes to dining preferences?

➤ According to your research, what pizza toppings do millennials really like or dislike?

➤ Talk about your restaurant industry background, and the industry award you won three years ago.

Use your past successes to create new successes in the future. If you were recently interviewed on a radio show or podcast, record five or six minutes of your best moments, post the video to YouTube, and send that link to producers.

Do not underestimate the power of simplifying this process for your host or producer. They will appreciate it, and they will remember it later down the line when they're pressed for a no-stress, convenient guest. You want them to open your email and breathe a sigh of relief: "This guy looks easy. Here are all the questions, here's all the work. There's nothing for us to do. Let's have him on the show."

I did an interview once with two hosts from Fox News. It was a two-segment interview—host #1 led the first segment, and host #2 led the second. The tape started rolling, host #1 interviewed me using six questions from my sample list, and then we cut to commercial. After the break, host #2 took over—*and he asked me the exact same six questions.*

These are famous news anchors. You almost certainly know their names. The three of us sat around the same little table, mere feet from one another, and these two managed to block each other out entirely. I had to answer the exact same questions twice in a row! It was unprofessional, but more importantly, it illustrates how heavily hosts rely on the sample questions you send their way. These lists are not superfluous—send them to every producer, every time.

Protip: Publicists are very good about sending question lists to radio and podcast producers. However, they seldom customize the sample questions for each show. That's where you will have an edge, if you take the time to listen to the programs, learn some things about the hosts, and customize the list of questions sent to each program.

CHAPTER 9

The advantages of snail mail

There is special value in sending a tangible pitch—something concrete that a producer can hold in his or her hands. There are several steps to making snail mail work for you:

1. First, send the program a heads-up email, letting the producer know that a physical envelope will follow.

2. Second, send the pitch materials in an envelope that will really stand out.

When it comes to choosing an envelope, memorability is key. Your envelope should be bright, ostentatious, and unforgettable. Choose colors like aqua, orange, red, green, or purple. It should be explosive.

Absolutely do not send materials in a standard manila envelope from Office Depot—what a snooze! The last thing you want to do is send something generic and forgettable. That's what everyone else does.

If you are utilizing the snail mail strategy, do it right. Go and have custom envelopes made—big ones, 9 by 11 inches. Slap your headshot on the front of it, color it bright red, and ensure that your recipients won't soon forget your name.

When the postal equivalent of a bright red balloon ends up in the mailbox, is the producer or host going to miss it? Will it get lost? Of course not!

Call the host or producer a week later and say, "Did you receive a bright red envelope two days ago in the mail? I'm that guy." He or she will remember that bright red envelope. It is a phenomenal way to stand out.

What's inside your red envelope? Your long bio, your short bio, a headshot, your sample questions, and a sample product (if you have one). Customize the contents according to your marketing goals:

➤ If you are an author, you're going to send a copy of your book.

➤ If you are a parenting expert, you're going to send a flyer, a blurb, or some promotional materials.

➤ If you're positioning yourself as a management guru, include a list of consulting clients or corporate speaking engagements.

Whatever your business is selling, give the producer a taste. Setting yourself apart from the manila masses will not only send your name to the top of producers' mail stacks, but it will also boost your chances of snagging follow-up interviews. Sear yourself into his or her memory. When a guest cancels the interview at the last minute, or when the producer is hard-pressed to fill a slot, that bright red envelope stuffed with ready-made sample questions will start to look real nice.

CHAPTER 10

Reaching out by phone

I've talked about hiring a publicist. I've talked about using social networks, search, and other online services to connect with hosts and producers. I've talked about the merits and pitfalls of email, and snail mail. Now, let's discuss good, old-fashioned telephone calls, and why they are an ideal (but sometimes unrealistic) way to secure PR coverage.

Your number one asset as a potential radio or podcast guest is your voice and the way you use it. It's all in your tone, your enthusiasm, and your eloquence. None of that comes across in an email or online ad. No matter how boisterous your font, no matter how overzealous your CAPS lock usage, there is no good way to effectively convey your energy and charm to recipients through text and visual appeals.

This distinction is important. The phone messages you leave for producers not only serve as a means of communication, but they also shine a preliminary spotlight on the entertainment value you bring to the table. The dynamism (or lack thereof) of your voicemail offers a sneak peek into your radio presence, and has tremendous potential to sway producers in your favor right off the bat. It's an unofficial audition of sorts.

Conversely, a lackluster, uncertain voicemail reflects very poorly on you as a potential interviewee. Use this message as an opportunity to demonstrate how interesting you'll be on their show. Show them just how great of a guest you are!

I have two valuable pointers about this telephone call:

➤ It should be scripted.

➤ It must be committed to memory.

Once you are satisfied with the content of your script, rehearse it. Then rehearse it again. And again. And again! The script should roll off your tongue without a single pause or stutter, without hasty peeks at notes or cheat sheets. Sounding natural and confident is the key here. **Until you reach this level of absolute comfort with your script, you are not ready to start making calls.**

My personal favorite way to nail down a script is by calling my own phone and leaving myself messages, practicing the whole thing six or seven times until the flow is flawless. This might sound a little crazy, but I'm totally serious.

The ease and energy of your pitch will determine whether or not you get on the program. You don't want to mess it up. You need a great script, you need to practice it, and the call should express your enthusiasm and expertise.

Part 4

Creating the pitch

CHAPTER 11

Basic dos and don'ts of pitch writing

In the next few chapters, I'll be focusing on the pitch—the messaging that you send to producers and hosts in hopes of getting on the air. The pitch includes the all-important hook—the actual eight- to ten-word spiel that lies at the core of your appeal.

Always make sure your pitch is relevant to the show you're pitching. A cooking show will not want to interview an expert on corporate law. This might seem like a no-brainer, but it's an extremely common mistake that can waste the time of everybody involved. Make sure to spend time researching the show to determine whether or not you truly are an appropriate guest.

When you address the host or producer during your pitch—and this is deceptively critical—**use his or her name**! I receive hundreds of emails that read, "Dear Sir," or "To Whom It May Concern," or "Dear Reader," and it is a massive turn-off. *So*, I think, *you want to be on my show, but you haven't even bothered to figure out what my name is?* It seems like a common courtesy. Those people do not receive an invitation onto my show.

Do not make this same mistake when reaching out to hosts or producers. They want a personalized email that shows some measure of care, some indication that the correspondence is more than the product of a mass email blast. Something like, "Dear Julia, I listened to the *24/7 Unstoppable Business Podcast* and think I would be a great guest—here's why." It's not hard!

The golden rule of pitch writing (this also applies to many different types of professional correspondence) is to be clear and brief. This is especially important when it comes to your hook.

Whether it's the subject line of an email or your first few words during a phone call, you must be clear and deliver your pitch right out of the gate. It is critical that your introduction explicitly conveys what you are talking about! Producers have neither the time nor the energy to wade through self-indulgent prefaces or meaningless fluff, so avoid meandering at all costs!

The body of your pitch should parallel this level of specificity. Make it three paragraphs, or no more than a hundred words. Tell them what you want to talk about, give them some proof that you will make a good guest, and move on. Do not inundate them with a two-page long email request, complete with an elaborate account of your life story, or irrelevant details.

So cut the fluff. You do not need to squeeze 10 different fonts into your pitch. You do not need to make every word a different color. You do not need to attach 10 different photos— one relevant picture should be more than enough. You do not need curlicues over your Ls and little hearts dotting your Is. I receive pitches like this all the time, and I can promise you, I delete them the second they appear in my inbox.

Less is more, folks. Fluff will get you nowhere.

One last great addition to your pitch is the inclusion of sample questions, as discussed in Chapter 8. It's really good to say, "Here are three or four of the questions that you might ask me," or "Here are three or four bullet points that typically come up in my interviews."

The 10 commandments of a great pitch (and hook)

Now that we've covered the basics of pitch writing, let's dive into specifics. Below is a list of 10 commandments for creating the perfect pitch and hook.

Commandment #1: **Your hook needs to be controversial.** The best thing you can do for a radio show or podcast is elicit some sort of controversy. A contentious hook is a fabulous way to stimulate this kind of conversation. Take my own personal slogan, for example. Ask any pedestrian on the street: "What is entrepreneurship all about?" Nine times out of ten, their response will include some or all of these three words: creativity, risk, passion.

So what's my controversial hook? I take the exact opposite stance:

> *"Entrepreneurship is NOT about creativity, risk, or passion!"*

It's counterintuitive. It's attention-grabbing. It's interesting. It's exactly the type of hook that's going to pique a producer's interest: "Wow, this guy doesn't think that entrepreneurship involves risk. I've got to hear more about that!"

So, make your hook interesting. It can be something that takes established thoughts, wisdom, or values. Anytime you do that, the chances of getting on the show are fantastic.

Commandment #2: Be broad. Try to ensure your hook appeals to as many listeners as possible. Solve a ubiquitous problem, something that everyone deals with.

Weight-loss businesses are a great example. Almost everyone battles weight problems at one time or another. If your pitch includes the line, "a proven way to make weight loss easier for everybody," you're already there. That applies to almost anybody! It's a home run. The line appeals to health shows, but also to any other programs whose listeners struggle with weight, including easy-listening shows, parenting shows, and cooking shows, et cetera. They all have reason to bite.

Commandment #3: Be new. Everyone loves novelty. I'm talking about a hook that says, "Great new method for storing fruits," or "Great new method to make your children more obedient." Any of these buzzwords or catchy terms—"new," "improved," "the thing that everyone's talking about,"—let the producer know that you have something interesting to say, but also something that they've never talked about.

Commandment #4: Bust a myth. This is one of my favorites. Rule number four utilizes the same strengths as rule number one—using listeners' preconceived notions as a foothold for intriguing, provocative discussions. Here's an example:

> *"The media insists that fracking is bad for groundwater. Well, I have proof that fracking is actually perfectly fine for groundwater, and will in no way harm your health."*

Again, it's counterintuitive, it's potentially inflammatory, and it forces people to look your way. Everyone will be amazed that you have the audacity to make public statements that so flagrantly contradict everything they've been told. That kind of outrage is what gets you on the air.

Commandment #5: Be different. If you're a teacher with belief A in a school full of teachers with belief B, emphasize that. If you conduct your entire math class in Spanish or use garbage can lids to teach science, highlight that in your pitch. If you're the guy that swam across the English Channel blindfolded, make sure that story is in there.

Point toward your idiosyncrasies however you can—if you are unique and unusual, people will want to hear your story. Position yourself against the mainstream.

Commandment #6: Emphasize your credentials whenever possible. Now, the word "credentials" often connotes some sort of academic accomplishment. It's the "look at how many letters I have behind my name" trick. And hey, those kinds of credentials are really great, especially if they are distinctive! If you have letters, use them. In some cases, the fact that you're a Harvard-educated Ph.D., will be enough to get you on the show.

But don't get discouraged if you don't have an impressive degree. There is far more to credibility than schooling. There is an equally salient and effective type of credential that will reinforce your potential as a wonderful guest. I like to call them, "Been there, done that" credentials. It can be anything cool or notable that you've accomplished.

Maybe you're the guy who climbed Mount Kilimanjaro. That's an interesting credential. Or, you were nominated for an Emmy award. That, too, is a credential. Perhaps you were the number-one real estate agent in the State of Georgia, or your book was on the best-seller list for 10 weeks in a row.

You get the idea. Credentials are anything that proves you're good at what you do. Make no mistake; these credentials hold weight. Any time you can slide those little brags in during your pitch, do it. It will really help.

Commandment #7: Be relevant to topical news stories. This is one of the most sure-fire strategies you can use to get on radio or podcast shows. Here's your hook: "Did you see what happened on the news yesterday? I can comment on that." It's very simple and to the point. If you have banking expertise, the pitch may start like this:

> *"Did you hear that the Federal Reserve decreased the savings rate required of banks, drastically altering the discount rate? I can come on your show and tell your listeners about how that will impact their mortgage payments."*

Tackling current events relevant to your field of expertise reflects well on your brand and the show alike. Hosts love this approach because it makes their shows seem topical, fresh, and in-vogue. It indicates to audiences that they are paying attention to the world around them.

Commandment #8: Hit them where it hurts. Put some emotion into the pitch. If you're an expert on bullying, say something like:

> *"Are you concerned that your child might be suffering emotional or physical abuse from classmates? Did you know that victims of bullying are 2 to 9 times more likely to consider self-harm than non-victims? I'm here to talk about telltale signs of bullying and how YOU can help your children."*

This pitch goes straight for the heart! I'm saying, "Tune in to my interview so that I tell you about this difficult issue and show you how to be a better parent!"

Appeals to emotion are very, very hard to ignore. They are ubiquitous on mass media. How many times have you turned on the evening news and heard something like this:

> *"Is a secret poison invading your house, harming your family and pets? Details at 11."*

And of course, the details don't actually air until 11:27, and when they do, it's something like, "Did you know that drinking an entire bottle of dish detergent is bad for you?" They're scaring the pants off of you to make you watch the entire TV show! It's a little bit tricky, a little bit dirty, but you know what? It works.

***Commandment #9:* Be passionate.** Media loves passionate guests. Hopefully, this book thus far has effectively conveyed my passion for entrepreneurship. I *am* extremely passionate about the topic—but I'm also trying to make this interesting for YOU! Do the same with your interviews. You may do 50 interviews in 50 days on the same topic, but your passion and enthusiasm should be as apparent in interview #50 as it was for interview #1. In Chapter 20, I have specific tips on how to make your voice sound more passionate.

***Commandment #10:* You're selling your hook—not your product.** These two things are different. Yes, your ultimate goal is to sell your book or your parenting system or whatever, but that shouldn't come across in your hook. Your hook is not, "I'm here to sell a parenting system." That's the worst hook ever! Your hook is, "I can teach anyone how to be a great parent in three days or less."

Don't talk about the product itself, talk about the hook.

CHAPTER 12

Pitch-perfect emails

"McGraw-Hill author—275 great interviews—Entrepreneurship is not about creativity, risk, or passion."

There it is. That's my hook. It's the subject line of all my pitch emails. Those 14 words are absolutely seared into my brain from years of repetition, and they probably always will be! Let's deconstruct them.

➤ **"McGraw-Hill author."** Right off the bat, these three words establish my credibility. One of the world's leading publishers decided my ideas were worth publishing. I know what I'm doing.

➤ **"275 great interviews."** More credibility! I know what I'm doing, and I'm good at it, too. With 275+ interviews on my track record, you know I'll give you a great interview.

➤ **"Entrepreneurship is *not* about creativity, risk, or passion."** This is an unorthodox stance in a world of copycat ideas. It's interesting and stands out from the crowd ... and will give the host a meaty topic to dig into.

These important aspects of my hook ensure that the person reading my email will immediately recognize me as an authority, an expert, and someone who's done this before. Those 14 words also summarize, in a succinct and straightforward way, the gist of what I'll be talking about on the show. It's controversial, counter-intuitive and the exact opposite of what everyone thinks.

So just in the subject line of my email, I have sent several powerful messages to my host or producer. I'm an expert. I'm credible. I've done this before, and I've got something sexy as hell to talk about. And all of that is just in my hook.

Now, let's tackle the actual body of your pitch email. Remember—research the recipient's name and use it! No "Dear Sir" or "Dear Madam" allowed here. Personal touches speak volumes.

> *Dear Kate,*
>
> *I have been studying your radio show/podcast. I listened to your compelling interview with Frank Rudd the other day, and I found it fascinating. I think I would make a great addition to your program, as my area of expertise is quite similar to Frank's—however, my thesis could not be more different. I believe anyone can be an entrepreneur if they forget about creativity, risk, and passion. I have done 275 interviews promoting this topic. CNN called me "The Simon Cowell of Small Business," and I was even featured in a UPS commercial. I believe I would be a great guest on the show, and I'd love to discuss this with you further. Please give me a call at your convenience—my number is _____.*
>
> *Thank you for your time,*
>
> *Jim Beach*

So what have I done here? After reading my email, the host and/or producer know some crucial information. They know who I am, and what I believe. They know I have paid legitimate attention to their show. They know I have researched what they talk about, and that I genuinely believe I'd make a valuable addition to the discussion. They know why I matter, why I'm important, and what we'll probably talk about on the show.

If you can sprinkle in some sample questions, that makes a really great final paragraph. It might read like this:

Some of the things I frequently talk about in interviews are:

> ➤ *How did you decide to start your first business?*
>
> ➤ *Is creativity important for entrepreneurs?*
>
> ➤ *Should you be passionate about your business?*
>
> ➤ *When is the best time to start a business?*

Now, the host/producer knows exactly what the interview will be about.

At the end, include a call to action:

> *"I would love to be a guest on your show—please give me a call at*
> _____."

This pitch will work. It is tried and true—I have tested it many times. But it is wise to keep multiple email pitches in rotation. Personally, I like to use a different pitch every weekend. My reasoning: Sometimes, a certain pitch just won't land with a particular producer. It is valuable to note these failures, and to make adjustments accordingly. If they didn't like your first shot send an alternate pitch next time.

This does not mean you need to overhaul your entire script every time somebody rejects your advances. Just pay attention, and measure your metrics. Using the methods in this book, my response rate averages 15-20%. If you're sending out 100 emails per day and your response rate is 4% or less, you probably should change your approach.

There is nothing wrong with experimentation—send 10 different pitches to 10 different producers and see what happens. The worst-case scenario? You'll try again next week, new and improved.

> **Protip:** Keep in mind that the size of your target shows will have a significant impact on your response rates. The bigger the show, the slimmer the likelihood that you'll get a response. This is where you will need to switch from emails to calls, no questions asked. Don't email an A-level program and scratch your head when they don't hit you back!

CHAPTER 13

Piggybacking your pitch on news or events

As mentioned earlier, tying your pitch to news or special events can be a very effective approach to getting on the air. When there's a white-hot piece of breaking news or an interesting event taking place, radio shows and podcasts seek out expert voices. Here are three tips that can make your pitch stand out:

Tip #1: **Stay on top of breaking news.** A fire decimates downtown. Two local businesses are embroiled in a huge legal dispute. The governor was just indicted. Amazon has just announced a new product line. All of these news items are prime opportunities for you to get on the air.

Email and call your list *immediately*! Tell them how you can add value to this story by bringing expertise or perspectives that can illuminate the topic. Timing can be the difference between securing airtime and losing it to the next person in line.

Tip #2: **Follow social media like a hawk.** If you have your eye on a particular program, follow that program's Twitter or Facebook account and keep abreast of content as it comes. What are the topics being discussed by program staff or their audiences? Is there a relevant topic or angle that you can connect to your pitch?

Respond to tweets on a daily basis, and make yourself a part of the program's online conversation. It shows that you are thoughtful and genuinely interested in the show—a nice way to charm producers and boost your chances of securing an interview.

Tip #3: **Create an awareness day for your industry.** This might sound corny, but it's one of my favorite little pitch techniques. It can work well for programs that don't discuss hard news, or for experts with certain types of creative or professional backgrounds.

There are all sorts of national and international awareness days out there that you probably don't know about—some are meaningful, some are silly as all get out, but all are observed in one way or another. There's National Brick Day (April 14th), World Laughter Day (1st Sunday in May), National Nurse Day (May 6th), National Toasted Marshmallow Day (August 30th), and countless others.

While National Toasted Marshmallow Day may seem like an unusual topic of conversation for a radio program, I can see it tied into all kinds of pitches. For instance, if you just published a book about hiking and other back-country activities, you could make a pitch to discuss end-of-summer camping trips, from National Toasted Marshmallow Day to Labor Day. Or, if you're involved in scouting, it could be part of a pitch about how parents can get their kids interested in joining a local troop.

Familiarize yourself with awareness days that pertain to your company, product, or mission, and think about ways of leveraging them to lend larger-scale importance to your pitch.

If there is no holiday that sufficiently relates to your business, make one up! There are loads of websites that allow you to designate certain calendar days as awareness days of your choosing. Google "create a new awareness day" to get started.

As the day in question approaches, email a producer on your target list with a pitch like this:

> *"Did you know that June 22nd is National Balloon Day? Well, I happen to have a great tie-in for that, a unique perspective on the balloon industry that I can talk about on your show."*

These events help make your talking points special and current—qualities that producers can't get enough of.

Part 5

Pre-interview preparation

CHAPTER 14

Know your host, know your audience

The host is your friend. Like any good friend, you not only need to know his or her name, but you also need to use it. This is an essential trick for a great interview—address the host by name at least once per minute. Say things like, "You know, Janet, that's an interesting point," or "I'm so glad you asked me that, Janet." People love it when you use their names—it melts away some of the ice and makes them feel important.

But you need to take it a step further. Don't stop with the name—gather concrete information about the host. I want you to know the book Janet published last year, I want you to know how Janet landed where she is today, and I want you to know who Janet interviewed on the show last week. Say things like, "Well, Janet, just like your book talks about ..." or, "As a former executive at Nestlé, Janet, you know this better than anybody," or, "As Phil Daniels mentioned on your show the other day ..."

That is gold, right there. Janet loves the fact that you're promoting her book. Janet loves the fact that you know who she is. Janet is going to invite you back to the show, guaranteed. These are the moves that will take you from a B-minus guest to an A-plus regular.

A second thing to focus on is the host's interview style.

Over the years, I have come to realize that my own interview style as a host tends toward quick-fire questions and responses. I typically spit out three or four interview questions at once, and I expect my guests to handle the deluge with ease. I assume that they have done some sort of preliminary research, such as looking at the website or listening to archived programs online, and that they are familiar with the way I do things.

My interview on the Rusty Humphries Show exemplifies the potential of preliminary research to seriously save your butt.

Rusty is an attack interviewer. He starts the program, introduces the guest, and asks a few simple, benign questions. He makes you feel safe ... and then he goes for the jugular!

Question number three is always designed to trip up guests, and to make them look bad. For instance, the title of my first book is *School for Startups*. The tagline at the bottom reads, "Guaranteed Success in 90 Days or Less." I didn't write that part. It was crammed down at the bottom of the front cover at the publisher's insistence, and to my dismay.

What do you think Rusty's third question was? "Ninety days, Jim? You can't make an entrepreneur in 90 days or less!"

But I had done my research, and knew what to expect on Rusty's program. I knew he was going to be harsh, and I came prepared with a great answer to anything he might throw my way.

Don't underestimate the importance of advance prep—it can keep a lot off egg off your face. An hour or two spent familiarizing yourself with the show's material could be the difference between a dazzling performance and an uncomfortable train wreck. Study up.

Demographics and regional considerations

It's critical to understand the audience and adjust your messages and stories accordingly. Take note of the show's demographics, and use that information to endear yourself to the audience and host. What works for a general-interest talk show may not go over with the audience of a sports podcast, based on gender, age, and other differences.

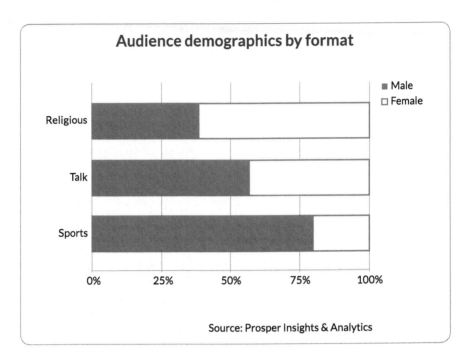

Source: Prosper Insights & Analytics

Beyond basic demographics, you will also want to appeal to cultural sensibilities. For instance, if you get on the Howard Stern show, you want to sound like a jerk. That's what his audience expects. If you're on a small show in the rural South, reign in the Brooklyn accent and try to sound a little more Southern.

Now, I'm not suggesting that you affect some fake persona as a pandering tactic, but be sensitive! If I'm doing an interview in Alabama, I will use the word, "y'all." If I'm doing an interview in Boston, I'll leave it out—"y'all" just doesn't sound right up North.

Protip: Make an effort to know your audience. A little common ground goes a long way.

CHAPTER 15

Respect the clock

The length of a radio interview typically depends on the duration of the show. Most shows run about an hour long, and there's usually about six minutes of commercial time. That leaves around 54 minutes of room for actual content, including the introductory spiel, on-air banter, reminders of upcoming programs, and other material that regularly appears in the show.

On an average hour-long program, you will encounter interviews of four different lengths, depending on how many guests are featured. There's the 6- to 8-minute interview, the 12-minute interview, the 22-minute interview, and the 45-minute interview. This is how the different formats work:

➤ **Six- to 8-minute interviews** are most common with large-scale, A-level shows that are strapped for time. Expect short, relatively shallow interviews with three to four questions at most. For these gigs, I often don't even bother sending the host my full 12–15 questions—he or she will only manage to cover a quarter of them in the allotted time. Instead, I select a handful of my favorite questions.

➤ **Twelve-minute interviews** are usually squeezed between two commercial breaks. Just like the 6- to 8-minute interviews, these don't allow for much meandering. They are brief and to-the-point. Again, it's a good idea to reduce the size of your questions list—pick a few of your zingers and leave it at that. Do not attempt to squeeze all 12–15 of your sample questions into a 12-minute interview—the segment will feel rushed and cursory. You want your interview to be focused and true to your talking points, so go for quality over quantity here.

➤ **Twenty-two-minute interviews** are my favorite. They are the most common on my own show. Most 22-minute segments run straight through without any commercial breaks, so be prepared to talk for the full stretch without stopping. This length tends to be an industry standard—you will run into more 22-minute interviews than any of the others. It is the ideal amount of time for our purposes.

➤ Finally, **45-minute interviews** are the longest and are relatively rare, as they essentially fill up an entire hour-long show. The duration is typically broken up by three or four commercial breaks, which means that you will be reintroduced three or four times.

Lengthier interviews give you considerably more wiggle room in terms of available time to hit all of the questions on your list, but don't overdo it. The following table shows what to expect, but keep in mind that some shows may have different formats or pacing.

Talk time (minutes)	Commercials/Interstitials	Questions
6–8	0	2–3
12	0	4–5
22	0–1	7–8
45	3-4	12+

Some important rules of thumb to keep in mind:

1. Never let an answer run on longer than a minute or a minute and a half—unless the host lets you keep talking (see Chapter 18, "It's all in the stories").

2. You should allow the host plenty of opportunities to interject with a follow-up question, a joke, or a point of clarification.

3. Don't turn your segment into a self-indulgent monologue—attention spans are short, and things will go stale fairly quickly.

4. It's important to keep things volleying back and forth.

5. Respect the clock—don't try to push beyond the allotted time.

When I am invited to an interview, the first thing I do is ask about the length of my segment. This allows me to organize my material ahead of time, map out my main ideas, and ensure that I send the producer/host all the appropriate information. It would be a shame if you jumped through all the right hoops, landed a nice interview, and then didn't manage to cover your talking points during the segment itself.

CHAPTER 16

Pre-show publicity

As a radio host, I judge my guests based on how much good they will do for my program and me.

Hosts not only want you on their shows because of your infotainment value, but also because of your contact list and follower base. They are hoping that you, as a courteous guest, will drive ratings for the show by publicizing your appearance to Facebook friends, LinkedIn connections, and Twitter/Instagram followers.

A great guest—the type of person who I invite back four or five times—is the guest who I see promoting the show in advance. This is part of the unspoken contract between us, the bargain between interviewer and interviewee. I'll scratch your back, you'll scratch mine, and then you'll tweet about our scratching session to all 10,000 of your eager followers. So, before you go on the show, make sure you spread the word!

There is an important exception to keep in mind: Some shows are pre-recorded a week or two in advance, and then the hosts pretend to air them live. If your "live" appearance is pre-recorded, take note! Don't spoil the illusion and publicize the interview two weeks before it's due.

James A. Beach
May 9, 2015 · ❸

Thanks John Livesay for having me on your show! great honor - learn to make a great elevator pitch!

Jim Beach | Successful Ways to Pitch

Jim Beach has successfully pitched the White House and has a radio show that plays on 11 FM stations called School for Startups.

SELLINGSECRETSFORFUNDING.COM

Work with the host and the program staff—shoot them an email asking when you should start tweeting about the segment. Should you retweet their tweets or share their Facebook posts? How can you work together to best achieve both of your goals? The host will be very impressed that you want to help build up the show itself in addition to promoting your brand. It's a great way to establish trust and increase the likelihood of a repeat invitation.

Protip: Ninety-nine percent of the time, you will not talk to the host until two seconds before you go on air. Don't expect to. Nothing screams "rookie" like guests emailing me ahead of time and asking for an introductory phone call before the segment.

Part 6

How to give a
great interview

CHAPTER 17

Romancing the host and maintaining the flow

Your pitch is successful, the producer has arranged for you to appear on the show, and your interview is about to start. Now it's time to get in the right frame of mind.

I want you to romance the host. Whether it's a man or a woman, and whether you're a man or a woman, you are there to flirt. You want to let the hosts know you think they are highly impressive, that the show is great, the guests are great, and that they ask great questions.

When one of the hosts asks you a question, start out by saying, "Wow, that's a great question, Brenda! No one's ever asked me that before!" Throw his or her name in there as much as possible—it's the verbal equivalent of steady eye contact.

All radio shows as well as many podcasts start the same way. The host introduces himself, gives an overview of the program, and maybe cracks a few jokes. "I'm really excited to introduce my next guest," he says. Then, he rattles off the bio you sent him, sings your praises, et cetera. Finally: "Jim, thanks for being with us!"

Your response should be some form of, "Thanks so much for having me on the show, Phil! It's an honor to be with you." These should be the first words out of your mouth, 100 percent of the time. Always thank the hosts for their time and for the opportunity to come on the show. Anything less comes across very poorly. After this little exchange, the host will ask the first question on your list, and the interview will be off and running.

Always remember that *you* are in control of this interview. You came on the show for a reason—to get through your talking points and promote your business—and that's exactly what you're going to do! Answer a question for 60 seconds, and then pause. If the host doesn't interject, keep going.

Don't be rude or interrupt hosts, of course—it's their show, after all. If they want to talk, let them. But if they don't butt in during your half-second lull, keep on plowing through your talking points. Don't stop until the host interrupts you.

Sometimes, you can go for six, twelve minutes without the host saying a word. That's okay! Getting your full message across is the whole point. So be prepared to rattle off your entire spiel with no help or interjections from the host. It happens more often than you'd think, and if you've done the right preparation, it makes a great interview.

If you reach the end of point number one and the host doesn't interject or ask a follow-up question, feel free to change the subject and jump to point number two. You are in charge here. Say something like, "Everything I just said about risk-taking is really important, but I also want to talk about creativity." Now you've changed the conversation topic and you're ready to move on to your next point on the list.

Always be ready to launch back into your question list. At some point, the host will inevitably veer off-topic. Maybe he thought some tangential comment you made was interesting, or perhaps he wants to ask an unrelated question that's not on your list. That's fine—but just be sure to answer his question quickly and succinctly.

Always return to your talking points as soon as you can. Remember, your question list is the definitive outline for this interview, not the host's whims or points of clarification. Avoid unnecessary tangents and stick to your list as closely as possible.

CHAPTER 18

It's all in the stories

People remember stories long after they have forgotten everything else. Regardless of whether the stories are funny or sad, heartbreaking or infuriating, those emotions lend information a special kind of staying power. People use stories to relate to each other and discover things about themselves.

If you want to really ingrain your point into the minds of your audience, wrap it in a story that's sure to be remembered and repeated. It's the best thing you can do to ensure retention of the material you want to convey. A great anecdote has that kind of potential.

Beyond information retention, it is important to always remember that as a radio or podcast guest, you are actually taking part in show business. After all, the core of radio (and podcasting) is quality entertainment. You are there to be entertaining and educational. Make your audience laugh, have fun, and be part of the show! And never lose sight of that fact, and never forget that keeping your audience engrossed is priority number one.

As any decent performer or artist knows, the beginning of an entertainment piece is of paramount importance. Whether it's the first chords of a song, the preface of a book, or the pilot of a TV show, the audience's attention must be captured in those first few moments. Failure to immediately hook audiences will result in that song being skipped, that book slamming shut, and that channel being changed. Radio is no different.

For this reason, fabulous opening anecdotes are a vital element of successful interviews. If you grab the audience's attention early on, if you touch their hearts from the get go, you're set. So that first story should be one of your best.

One of the best ways to accomplish this is by pushing emotional buttons. If you can make people laugh, do it. If you can make people cry, even better! Talk about the emotional roller-coaster of something happening with your company.

For example, my wife runs an Amazon business. She has grown her revenue from $500 to almost $50,000 in one year. That's a fascinating story in itself, but I inject emotion into it by discussing the amazing impact my wife's business has had on her self-esteem, and how much she's grown as a person. I am genuinely proud of her and her success, and that passion is unmistakable when I tell the story on air.

If I bring out the big guns within the first 60 seconds of my segment, it's basically guaranteed that the host will love it, that the audience will love it, and that both will be wrapped around my finger for the remainder of the interview. Plant your best material at the beginning, and the payoff will last until you hang up the phone.

Protip: When preparing for an interview, for each question on your sample sheet, come up with two brief stories that reinforce your point. You won't necessarily be able to tell all of them, especially if your interview is on the shorter side, but it's excellent practice for longer segments. Anecdotes wake the audience up; they give listeners something relatable to grab hold of. You can never brainstorm too many.

CHAPTER 19

Promotion and cross-promotion

You're on the show to promote something—a product, a service, a brand, or an idea—so make sure you promote it! Whatever it is you're trying to sell, mention it once every three minutes, regardless of whether the host asks about it.

If you're a gardening expert and the host asks, "What's the most important part of gardening?" You can answer with, "Well, Barbara, as I talk about in my new gardening book, *The Joy of Urban Gardening*, the most important part of gardening is ..."

About once every three minutes is the sweet spot. It gets your point across and helps your product stick in listeners' heads without sounding desperate or blatantly promotional.

You should also use your interview as an opportunity to cross-promote. If you've published a gardening book, odds are you also sell other gardening-related products—gardening supplies, gardening classes, et cetera. Cross-promotion can also extend to your personal brand and any noteworthy aspects of your career.

In addition to my radio show and writing career, I travel the world as a keynote speaker. One of my favorite places to present is India Institutes of Technology—a group of exclusive universities scattered across the country. I am invited to speak at IIT fairly often, and I love to casually namedrop that fact whenever I get a chance on-air. I like to say things such as, "Well, you know Bob, I just got back from presenting over at IIT in India ..." Cue anecdote.

These little cross-promotional stories accomplish several things for my brand. First, they make me seem pretty important. It's not every day you get flown across the globe to speak to some of the world's greatest young minds.

Perhaps more importantly, the anecdotes promote parts of my broader career that wouldn't necessarily come up otherwise. After that anecdote, the audience is aware of my clout as a speaker, they are aware that there are other things they can purchase from me. Maybe somebody listening will want to hire me as a lecturer!

Don't limit yourself exclusively to the one product that got you on the air—use your interview time broadly and wisely. The following examples show how to leverage cross-promotional dynamics in various topic areas.

Interview topic	Product to cross-promote	Service to cross-promote
Pizza for millennials	Pizzeria & home delivery	Catering
Maritime history	Maritime antique shop	Waterfront tours
Exercise for diabetics	Workout videos	Physical therapy services
College admissions	SAT prep book	Counseling for students
Social media marketing	Online lessons	Brand consulting

For instance, if you're on the air to talk about college admissions, not only can you bring up your new SAT guidebook, but you can also mention your counseling services for teens and their families.

CHAPTER 20

Nine tips to sound great

As a guest, it is essential that you pay attention to audio quality. This often-overlooked issue can make or break your interview.

Tip #1: Use a decent phone

In the olden days, hosts required guests to call in via POTS—plain old telephone service, otherwise known as a landline. Calling from newfangled, unpredictable cell phones was highly frowned upon.

The reason behind this rule was audio quality. Cell phone signals could sound garbled, introduce long delays, or include other unwanted sounds.

One time, a guest had the nerve to call in to my show from a moving convertible. I couldn't make out a word he said—just the whoosh of the wind and something that sounded a little like "Aaarghgh!"

These days, if a guest calls me and the audio quality is poor, I simply refuse to conduct the interview. **If you don't care enough to call me from a decent telephone, you clearly don't deserve to be on my show.** Don't be that person!

That said, the latest generation of smartphones has largely eliminated the necessity of POTS-based interviews. Newer iPhones actually have built-in noise reduction capability—a microphone on the back of the device records and reduces ambient noise, removing it from the phone's audio signal. In my experience, these phones produce even better call quality than landlines.

When asked whether I'm calling from a POTS, I have historically lied into my iPhone—"Yeah, I am. How's my signal?" They say, "You sound great!" Assuming you have a newer-model iPhone or a high-end Android device, you will probably do just fine calling from your smartphone. If you are using an older device or a cheapo phone, you have a greater risk of audio problems during an interview—and irritating the host.

Tip #2: The interview should take place in a quiet, stable environment.

The ideal place to conduct an interview over the phone is in a quiet place with no visual or auditory distractions.

Not everyone has easy access to such locations, however. I do most of my interviews from home, where my two massive Dobermans scamper around at all hours of the day, whimpering and slobbering to no end. I also have a toddler son who likes to run around and tackle me whenever he thinks it's funny. I have done interviews while literally running around my house, trying to hide from dogs and children, desperate to find a quiet spot where I won't be interrupted.

Don't be like me. Find a quiet spot in advance where you can have a decent telephone call free of distractions. Avoid moving convertibles, enormous canines, and hyperactive children. Any background noise from the office, the coffee shop, or the television will make you look incredibly unprofessional.

Tip #3: Have a glass of water nearby at all times.

Hydration will refresh your throat and make your voice sound better. Take a sip while the host is talking so that your answer will be clear and smooth, free of any coughs or scratchiness.

Tip #4: Put on a happy face.

This piece of advice to improve audio quality might sound a little silly, but it works. I want you to smile during the entire interview.

As any decent cold-caller will tell you, smiling actually makes your voice sound better. You sound more energetic. You probably *are* more energetic! Remember, radio is all about the charisma and enthusiasm you convey through speech, so it is essential to do everything you can to maximize the quality of your delivery.

Tip #5: Animate your voice and improve intonation

People constantly ask me how I improve my vocal performance, and how I make my voice sound bright and interesting on air. Here is my secret: Go buy a children's book, and read it out loud.

I have four children, so I am a well-seasoned storybook reader. If you have ever read aloud to a child, you know that inflection is the name of the game—silly noises, scary noises, or wacky noises, as the situation demands.

> *"'Aaargh!' the Cyclops cried. "Who stole my cookies from the cookie jar?!"'*

If your voice doesn't rise and fall and grumble in your chest while you read that sentence aloud, it'll be a thumbs-down from tiny audience members. Making your voice animated is critical for keeping listeners engaged and entertained. This holds true for people of all ages. Practicing intonation with silly kid's books will help make your voice richer and livelier—qualities that translate into a great radio interview.

Tip #6: Show your passion

On a similar note, make sure your passion comes across in your delivery. There's nothing worse than listening to monotonous drawl from someone who just doesn't seem interested in what they're talking about. I wouldn't listen to that person, and I don't want them on my show. So be as excited and energetic as possible. Show us that you care about the subject.

Tip #7: Stand tall

Another tip that can make a real difference in the way you sound to hosts and audiences: Stand during your interview. Sitting collapses the diaphragm and constricts airflow, diminishing the power of your vocal delivery. Standing also increases blood circulation and energy, giving your voice that extra zing and enhancing performance quality. Walking around helps, too. You will sound better and your interview will be more dynamic. Smile, stand, and stroll around!

Tip #8: Take notes

Next, have a pen and paper ready. Even for experienced interviewees, questions can come hard and fast. Keeping all that information straight in your head is very difficult, and if you are not prepared, the host and audience will hear a lot of stammering and stuttering.

So you will have to take notes at some point. Be prepared to jot down questions as they come, points you want to bring up later, et cetera. I almost always find that having a pen and paper handy has a significant positive impact on the quality of my interviews.

Tip #9: Make the most of studio appearances

In my career of 275 interviews, only about 10 were conducted in person. Call-ins are far more prevalent. If you live in major media hubs like New York City or Los Angeles, studio interviews might be more commonplace, but even that idea operates under the assumption that your target shows will be local—the majority of programs will be spread out across the country. Nevertheless, it's worth sharing some important pointers about studio interviews.

First, arrive at the studio early—about fifteen minutes before the scheduled time should do the trick. This is not only professional and polite, but it also soothes any anxieties the producer might have about a no-show guest. Nothing scares the pants off of program staff like deserters.

Dress casually and comfortably—blue jeans are just fine. Radio stations usually have very laid-back work environments, so skip the suit and tie.

That said, bring a jacket just in case the AC is blasting. I have shivered my way through several interviews, so learn from my mistakes! Chattering teeth don't exactly scream, "star power."

Bring the host a copy of your book, a product sample, or any other promotional materials you have on hand. It's a thoughtful gesture that promotes your business long after the interview's conclusion!

Protip: If you do a studio interview, be sure to snap a few selfies in front of the microphone, ideally with the station logo visible in the background. If possible, ask someone on staff to take a photo of the interview itself. These photos will make important additions to your social media profile and future pitches alike.

Part 7

The aftermath

CHAPTER 21

The post-show carrot

Most interviews end with the following dialogue: "We had a great time talking with you, Jim. How can our listeners get in touch with you?"

At this point, I will offer up my website URL, my Twitter handle, and maybe my Facebook page. And then the interview is over. Weeks go by, and nothing changes. My sales don't increase. What did I do wrong?

Let's think about this for a second. According to the techniques taught in Marketing 101, it takes three or four "touches" to sell somebody. The average somebody is unlikely to buy your product after hearing your pitch once. It takes more touches!

But the nature of radio and podcasting makes this a tad bit more complicated. If you don't take the proper steps, your interview will end and innumerable potential customers might be lost to the ether. Short of calling the station and begging for listeners' email addresses, how do you reel people in and make it to that third or fourth touch?

The answer lies in the very last part of your segment, just before the host clicks "Stop Recording." You must lure listeners to your website with a specific call to action:

> "Wow, thanks for having me on your show. I really appreciate your time. I would love it if your listeners visited my website at www. SchoolForStartups.com. If they type in their email, I'll mail them something for free!"

This carrot at the end of the segment is the key to success. It will drive listeners to your site and force them to enter their email addresses in return for the first chapter of your book, a free sample of your product, or some other item of interest or value. It's an incredibly critical and effective way to capture customers' interest and gather contact information while simultaneously securing open-ended potential for follow-up marketing. Entice them with goodies now, market to them for years.

CHAPTER 22

How to handle the "cool-down"

At the end of every show, after recording has ceased, there is a brief "cool-down" period. This is the part where the host thanks you again off the air, maybe banters with you a little. The "cool-down" is a short but precious networking resource—use this time to ask the host or producer if they have contacts or recommendations for other shows that might like to interview you.

As someone in the radio world, I know hundreds of other hosts in the same space as me. If a guest of mine came on the show, did a great interview, and then asked me during our concluding banter, "Hey, would you hook me up with some of your friends?" I would be more than happy to oblige, especially if the interview was of high quality.

Using this method, I got one show host to introduce me to five others—all of whom ended up inviting me onto their own programs. One of these five was Melinda Emerson, a small-business writer for the *New York Times*.

Entrepreneurship PR doesn't get much better than that, and I made it happen by bantering with someone else down the stream. Never hang up the phone without doing some networking.

The repeat guest

After you've completed a great interview, nine times out of ten the host will graciously offer, "We'd love to have you back."

Frequently, this is no more than standard protocol—a courteous sendoff as empty as it is polite. They're saying that because it's expected, not because they necessarily intend to extend a second invite.

But it doesn't have to stop there. There are plenty of opportunities to make this formality a reality and secure a future slot on the show. If you were good the first time around, they're going to want you back—but it's usually up to YOU to make it happen.

Most interviews take place over the phone. At the end of the interview, the host will typically disconnect, and you're put back through to the executive producer. The producer's post-segment task is to say, "Thanks for coming on. That was great. Can you make sure to send me your headshot and your bio and all that?" It's the logistics stuff.

It's also your opening. Take this time to tell the producer:

> *"Thanks a lot for having me on the show. I really enjoyed it. Please let me know if you ever have a cancellation and are pressed to fill an empty slot. If you ever need a guest within five minutes' notice, I'm your guy. I just wanted to let you know that."*

What you've done here is plant an extremely important seed in the producer's mind. If there's ever a cancellation or emergency, he knows that YOU are a person he can call to save the day. As a radio host with 14 different guests per week, I can personally attest to the enormous value of this little seed, and the likelihood that your planting it will eventually put you back on that program.

On average, three guests cancel on me every week. So that's three holes *per week* that I am unfortunately tasked with filling at the very last minute. There is never advance notice—nobody ever calls three days beforehand. They call ten minutes beforehand, if I'm lucky. And I am left scrambling to fill that empty space as quickly as possible without compromising the quality of my guests.

Now, if only there was somebody out there whom I could call at a minute's notice. Somebody whom I know is a reliably entertaining and informative guest. Somebody game to appear on my show at the eleventh hour. Somebody like ... you!

The fantastic utility of this little post-show conversation with the producer doesn't stop at last-minute cancellations. You can plant another seed to help you capitalize on the distinct value of your particular area of expertise. Remind the executive producer and the host exactly what you specialize in, and emphasize your potential for future expert commentary. Say something like:

> *"Hey, next time a politician gets caught in an ethics-based scandal, keep me in mind. I happen to be an ethics professor, and I think I'd be a great fit for the segment."*

Again, you have planted a seed bursting with promise. Corruption scandal rears its head? They know whom to call. You're an expert on Boeing's global business, and drama strikes the airline industry? They know whom to call.

That is the crux of what we are trying to accomplish here. We want to sear your name into the executive producer's mind. Our goal is to ensure that the next time a producer or host is left desperate for a guest, they think of *you*.

I have appeared on hundreds of different shows as a guest. Approximately half asked me back for additional interviews. Many have invited me back on four or five different occasions. One show was so impressed with my performance that they promptly invited me back—for six months! That's right, I appeared on the show every single Friday for half a calendar year. My segment eventually became a standard feature on the show. And it all happened because I planted that seed.

> **Protip:** This strategy will continue to bear fruit long after your 15-second conversation with the producer. Always shoot for that repeat guest slot—it is a gift that keeps on giving.

Post-interview steps

We've reached the end of the road. You made it! You found tons of great radio and podcast shows to target, wrote the perfect pitch, connected with producers galore, and nailed the interview.

But you're not quite done. In this chapter, I want to outline the post-interview steps you should take to maximize the impact of your time on-air.

I've already discussed publicizing your radio and podcast appearances in advance, but doing so after the fact is even more essential. Once the interview airs, be very aggressive with your social media. Tweet the link on Twitter, post it on Facebook, share it on LinkedIn—the works. You want the segment to live forever.

Beyond these social media basics, however, you need to start building a strong media page on your website. An easily accessible tab on your site should list all the media interviews you've ever done, every article that has ever quoted your expert opinion. Be sure to include working links to each piece and a little icon with the show's logo.

The media page is essential for establishing credibility and impressing future producers. It will show that you are a professional who knows what you're doing. And of course, this little collection of shout-out links makes great PR for them, too. They will want to be added to your list.

Lastly, it is important that you make the most of those listener emails you collected from your end-of-show action offer. At best, you will send these people a copy of your book or a free sample of your product. But at the very least, you should send them an email expressing gratitude for their time and attention.

Protip: If you collect a hundred emails in the two or three days following an interview, it's safe to say that those hundred people are responding positively to your material. Shoot them a message that thanks them and says, "I noticed you." Those are the sorts of gestures that help cultivate long-term relationships with your customer base and make the most out of your time on-air.

CHAPTER 24

The long haul

More than 7 years after that first tentative Google search on my sofa, I'm still leveraging free radio and podcast marketing opportunities. Let me tell you from personal experience—once you start, you'll never want to stop. It's an addiction. It's easy, it's incredibly lucrative, and it's just fun.

More important than all that, though, is the multiplicity of benefits that my work as a radio and podcast guest continues to produce.

This business keeps my skills sharp. With every new audience comes a fresh opportunity to hone my expertise as a conversationalist, as a salesman, and as a storyteller. I never get sick of it.

My appearances are also a fantastic way to test new material, whether it be anecdotes, jokes, taglines, or pitches. I have a few different books in the works right now, and I love using radio and podcasts as an opportunity to experiment with the content I'm working on.

Finally, and perhaps most importantly, radio and podcast appearances keep my books moving off the shelves, and money flowing into my pocket.

So, this is my final piece of advice: I want you to plan on doing this for an hour per day, every day, for the rest of your career. That's pretty serious commitment, but in the end, you'll get what you (don't) pay for. Get ready.

At this stage in the game, securing slots on radio shows and podcasts requires fairly minimal energy on my part. Almost inevitably, at least one invitation rolls in per week, and that's without much effort from my end. Generally speaking, I tend to devote two or three hours to this system every weekend—but that's after 7 years. As I've mentioned throughout the book, radio marketing eventually becomes self-perpetuating, and I'm very much enjoying life on the other side of that bridge.

Seven years on the job, and where am I now? That's right—still on my sofa. With my wife and kids beside me, and two massive Dobermans at our feet.

A message from the authors

Thanks for taking the time to read *Free Radio & Podcast Marketing In 30 Minutes*. This guide distills our experience hosting, producing, and taking part in hundreds of interviews. We hope our advice will help you leverage radio and podcast marketing to further your own business, brand, or idea.

We also have a special request: After you have read the book, could you spend a few minutes to review it online? Honest reviews let other readers know what to expect and help raise the book's profile.

Finally, as a small thank-you for purchasing this book, we want to make available to you Jim's list of more than 2,000 names of executive producers and hosts described in Chapter 7! Email james.beach@att.net to get a copy of the list, or to ask any questions you may have about this book and/or getting on the radio. There are additional resources available at schoolforstartupsradio.com.

Thanks again for your interest!

Jim Beach and Rachel Lewyn

About the authors

Jim Beach

Jim Beach is an experienced author, broadcaster, educator, and entrepreneur. Jim's first book, *School for Startups* (McGraw-Hill, 2011) was a top-ten title on Amazon, and his small business radio show, School for Startups Radio, airs on AM/FM stations across the United States and online.

At the age of 25, Jim started the American Computer Experience and grew the company with no capital infusion to $12 million in annual revenue and more than 700 employees. After the business was acquired in 2001 for $200 million, Jim taught at Georgia State University and was the top-ranked business school instructor for 12 consecutive semesters.

In addition to hosting his own radio show, Jim has also appeared on the other side of the microphone as a frequent media guest and commentator. Dubbed the "Simon Cowell of venture capital" by CNN, he has been interviewed by NPR, MSNBC, and the *New York Times*.

Rachel Lewyn

Rachel Lewyn studies anthropology at Emory University in her hometown of Atlanta, Georgia. A former producer for School for Startups Radio, she handled all aspects of screening potential guests and coordinating interviews. As a contributing writer for FanBolt.com, Rachel was responsible for creating search-optimized news articles about cinema, television, and pop music.

Index

V

voice, 23, 43, 51, 77–78
voicemail, 43
    scripts, 44

W

websites, 1, 3, 10, 26, 28, 30, 34, 39,
        61, 82, 87

Y

YouTube, 40

What readers are saying about IN 30 MINUTES® guides:

LinkedIn In 30 Minutes

"This was an excellent primer for someone like me who had a LinkedIn account but didn't really use it except to look up people."

"Since reading this a week ago, I have had more quality business interactions on LinkedIn than I have had in the last 2 years."

Genealogy Basics In 30 Minutes

"This basic genealogy book is a fast, informative read that will get you on your way if you are ready to begin your genealogy journey or are looking for tips to push past a problem area."

"The personal one-on-one feel and the obvious dedication it took to boil down a lot of research into such a small book and still make it readable are the two reasons I give this book such a high rating. Recommended."

Crowdfunding Basics In 30 Minutes

"Very understandable and absorbing. A must-read for any entrepreneur."

"On the verge of launching a crowdfunding campaign myself, this book has made me re-think my plans and my strategy. Take a step back and get the advice of someone who's been there."

Twitter In 30 Minutes

"A perfect introduction to Twitter. Quick and easy read with lots of photos. I finally understand the # symbol!"

"Clarified any issues and concerns I had and listed some excellent precautions."

Google Drive & Docs In 30 Minutes

"I bought your Google Docs guide myself (my new company uses it) and it was really handy. I loved it."

"I have been impressed by the writing style and how easy it was to get very familiar and start leveraging Google Docs. I can't wait for more titles. Nice job!"